MILITARY ENGINEERING
☆ ☆ ☆ ☆ ☆
IN ACTION

ARMORED TANKS

BATTLEFIELD DOMINANCE

Taylor Baldwin Kiland and Gerry Souter

Enslow Publishing
101 W. 23rd Street
Suite 240
New York, NY 10011
USA

enslow.com

Published in 2016 by Enslow Publishing, LLC.
101 W. 23rd Street, Suite 240, New York, NY 10011

Library of Congress Cataloging-in-Publication Data

Kiland, Taylor Baldwin, 1966–
    Armored tanks : battlefield dominance / Taylor Baldwin Kiland and Gerry Souter.
        pages cm. — (Military engineering in action)
    Includes bibliographical references and index.
    Summary: "Describes the development, use, and abilities of armored tanks in the military"—
    Provided by publisher.
    Audience: Grades 7-8.
    ISBN 978-0-7660-6908-4 (library binding)
    ISBN 978-0-7660-7059-2 (pbk.)
    ISBN 978-0-7660-7060-8 (6-pack)
    1. Tanks (Military science)—United States—Juvenile literature. 2. Armored vehicles, Military—Juvenile literature. I. Souter,
Gerry. II. Title.
    UG446.5.K446 2015
    355.8'3—dc23
                                    2015011216

Printed in the United States of America

Portions of this book originally appeared in *Battle Tanks: Power in the Field*.

Photo Credits: Chung Sung-Jun/Getty images News/Getty Images, p. 33; Co Rentmeester/The LIFE Picture Collection/Getty Images
p. 29; DoD photo by Staff Sgt. Shane A. Cuomo, US Air Force, p. 36; Ernest Brooks/ Wikimedia Commons/ British Mark I male tank
Somme 25 September 1916.jpg/Public Domain, p. 12; Guy J. Sagi/Shutterstock.com, p. 15; Heather Graham-Ashley, Sentinel News
Editor/courtesy DVIDS, p. 44; iurii/Shutterstock.com, p. 1 (right); Jared DeCinque/E+/Getty Images, p. 45; JEWEL SAMAD/AFP/Getty
Images, p. 9; JUNG YEON-JE/AFP/Getty Images, p. 7; Karl Gehring/The Denver Post via Getty Images, p. 28; Le Do/ Shutterstock.com,
p. 2; MSGT. J.W. HAYES/Wikimedia Commons/Marines-tank-Korea-19530705.JPEG/Public Domain, p. 21; PhotoQuest/Archive Photos/
Getty Images, p. 20; Randy Jolly/Timepix/The LIFE Images Collection/Getty Images, p. 26; Rich Koele/Shutterstock.com, p. 1 (left);
ROMEO GACAD/AFP/Getty Images, p. 17; Scott Nelson/Getty Images News/Getty Images, p. 23; Scott Olson/Getty Images News/Getty
Images, p. 4; Shutterstock.com (art/backgrounds throughout book): Dianka Pyzhova, Ensuper, foxie, kasha_malasha, pashabo; Staff
Sgt. M.D. Masters/US Department of Defense/Wikimedia Commons/DM-SC-92-03658.jpg/Public Domain, p. 19; Staff Sergeant James
Harper Jr., United States Air Force/ Wikimedia Commons/Colt M4 MWS Carbine Iraq.jpg/Public Domain, p. 42; US Air Force photo by
Tech Sgt. Francisco V. Govea II, p. 35; US Army photo, p. 6; US Army photo by Sgt. Chad Menegay, p. 30; US Army photo by Staff Sgt.
Stacy L. Pearsall, p. 8; US Marine Corps photo by Lance Cpl. Alexander Quiles, p. 37.

Cover Credits: Shutterstock.com: foxie (series logo), iurii (soldiers, front right), kasha_malasha (camouflage background), Le Do
(tank, back), Rich Koele (tank, front left).

CONTENTS

In the desert of Afghanistan, a private stands atop a Stryker vehicle after a live-fire exercise.

Stryker Brigades: Light and Lethal

They drove right into the line of fire. On a summer day in August 2009, ten Stryker Infantry Carrier Vehicles clipped along at 20 miles per hour (32 kilometers per hour) across the hot and dusty desert. They entered the town of Buyana in the Shah Wali Kot District of Afghanistan, about 25 miles (40 km) north of Kandahar. While the Strykers had been used in combat in Iraq since 2003, this was the first time they were to be tested in combat in Afghanistan. With news that Taliban insurgents were gathering in this town, the Stryker brigade was called to find them and drive them out of town.

As they entered the city limits, the soldiers inside the Stryker vehicles could clearly see the insurgents firing their weapons from nearby rooftops and windows. The ten vehicles moved into a "V" formation and started their attack, raining machine gun fire and

These Stryker vehicles are equipped with Warfighter Network Information-Tactical (WIN-T) systems.

grenades into the buildings while small groups of soldiers streamed out from the vehicles to engage more closely. Those who stayed inside the Strykers continued their assault. Surprised and overwhelmed by the force and rapidity of the attack, the insurgents fled town.

Twenty-First-Century Army

At the beginning of the twenty-first century, the US Army was looking for a new vehicle that could carry more soldiers and was better protected than the M113 armored personnel carrier or the M2 Bradley Fighting Vehicle. It also needed to be lighter than a tank and able to be transported on an aircraft. The Stryker was born. It was part of the army's new capability goal to deliver a brigade anywhere in the world in 96 hours, a division in 120 hours, and five divisions in 30 days. But this goal of getting the troops more quickly to remote battlefields was not a new one.

In World War II, "halftracks" were used to accompany tanks and move infantry soldiers to the battlefield. These halftrack vehicles were open-top trucks with caterpillar tracks instead of rear tires. Eventually, the army introduced fully tracked vehicles to navigate the rugged terrain of most battlefields.

The Stryker: Protected and Deployable

First deployed to Iraq in 2003, the Stryker Armored Vehicle is named for two soldiers who posthumously received the Medal of Honor: Specialist Robert F. Stryker, who received the award in Vietnam, and Private First Class Stuart S. Stryker, who received the award in World War II. It was developed out of a need for a vehicle that was heavy and lethal but well protected and easily deployable. It is the first new military vehicle to enter service into the US Army since the Abrams tank in the 1980s. The Stryker can be transported by a C-130 transport plane. In 2015, these vehicles were outfitted with the Warfighter Network Information-Tactical (WIN-T), a system that brings improved voice, video, and data communications to the front lines.

The Stryker Light Armored Vehicle (LAV)

LENGTH: 22 feet, 10 inches (7 m)
WIDTH: 8 feet, 11 inches (2.7 m)
HEIGHT: 8 feet, 8 inches (2. 6 m)
WEIGHT: 19–26 tons (17–24 metric tons)
SPEED: 60 miles per hour (96.6 kph)
RANGE: 300 miles (483 km) on one tank of fuel
CREW: Varies, but usually two
ARMOR: 14.5mm-resistant

MAIN ARMAMENT: Protector M151 Remote Weapon Station with 0.50-cal M2 machine gun, 7.62mm M240 machine gun, or MK-19 automatic grenade launcher
UNIT COST: $4.9 million (as of 2012)

Tank Column and Crew

A fast-moving group of tanks, called a column, provides rapid, high-explosive firepower. A "Thunder Run" column, so called because of the sounds made by the moving tanks, is made up of eight tanks. There are two platoons of four tanks each. Each platoon has a platoon leader. The platoon leaders are helped by a platoon sergeant and two tank commanders. On each of the four tanks in a platoon there is a tank commander, a gunner, a loader, and a driver. Each of these soldiers has a special job.

The tank commander is the leader and gives orders to the tank's crew. The tank commander selects targets and the type of ammunition to be fired at the target. The tank commander also communicates with the other tanks in the platoon.

The gunner, who sits to the right of the main gun, operates the turret and aims and fires the gun. Standing to the left of the main gun, the loader selects a heavy shell from the tank's protected storage space and shoves it into the rear of the gun's barrel, called the breech. The loader closes the breech, and the gun is ready to be fired. The driver controls the direction and speed of the tank while lying back almost all the way flat in a reclining chair located in the front of the tank's hull.

This sergeant directs a convoy of M1A2 Abrams tanks.

Inside a tank, a US soldier mans a gun while on the way to conduct a mission in Baghdad.

"Buttoning Up" a Tank

When a tank's crew gets ready to go into battle, they "button up" the tank. All the tank's hatches, or openings, are closed and locked for protection. Inside the hot, stuffy, buttoned-up tank, the instruments glow, the air-conditioning hums, and the engine howls like a huge vacuum cleaner.

To see outside, the crew uses vision blocks, periscopes that peer out through very thick glass. However, the glass is often dirty with dust or mud. The tank's driver is lying back in a reclining seat at the front and steering with the T-bar, which is similar to bicycle handlebars. The driver cannot see anything if there are bushes or other objects in front of the tank. The gunner has only the very narrow field of his gun sight to see through, and the loader sees nothing. Since he is higher in the turret with his periscopes, the tank commander can see more.

The History of Tanks

In World War I (1914–1918), soldiers fought from deep, wide trenches. The British developed tanks that rolled across the trenches and over sharp barbed wire. They helped the British soldiers stop opposing forces and created a barrier from opposing soldiers' fire. Their German opponents had never seen anything like these huge steel boxes, firing guns in all directions. Petrified by this new weapon, the German soldiers ran from their trenches.

Later, in World War II (1939–1945), the Germans built better tanks, using them to quickly defeat Poland and France. Their opponents, the Allied forces (including the United States), sent thousands of new tanks to fight the Germans. America's best tank at that time was the M4 Sherman. Its main gun was smaller than the German tanks' cannons, but there were more Sherman tanks to fight each German tank. By the time the Allies won World War II, they had learned a lot about building and fighting with tanks.

How Did the Tank Get Its Name?

"Tank" was a secret word used by the British in World War I to mean a vehicle that ran on treads instead of wheels. It was armed with cannons and machine guns and protected by steel armor. The British company that made the vehicles also made water tanks. The crates that contained the vehicles when they were shipped to France to be used in the war against Germany had "tank" painted on the sides to hide what was really inside. The name stuck.

This early model British tank, named C-15, had a wire grenade shield and a steering tail. Neither of these features were on the next models.

What Are the Parts of a Tank?

Most battlefield weapons used by individual opposing soldiers—such as rifles, machine guns, and small bombs called grenades—cannot stop a tank.

Turret

Most of the early tanks of World War I had cannons, but they were attached to the body, or hull, of the tank. The whole tank had to be aimed at the gun's target. Beginning with World War II designs, the tank's main gun was built into a turret. A turret is a small tower made of armored steel attached to the top of the hull that can turn in a complete circle. The main gun can be aimed and fired at a target ahead, to the side, or behind the tank, even while the tank is moving.

Three members of a tank's crew work in the turret. They are the tank commander, gunner, and loader. The turret contains all the tank's guns, big and small. Besides the big main gun, usually one or two smaller machine guns are attached to the top of the turret. One of these machine guns is sometimes mounted in a smaller turret atop the main turret. This mini-turret, or cupola, is usually operated by the tank commander. It gives him protection when he is being shot at by the opposing side. The other machine gun attached to the top of the turret is operated by the loader.

Sticking out of the turret next to the main gun is a light 7.62 millimeter (mm) machine gun fired by the gunner from inside the tank. This gun is used for smaller targets and shoots in the same direction as the main gun as the turret rotates.

Radio antennas are also attached to the turret to keep the commander connected to the other tanks in the platoon. One of these antennas is a Global Positioning System (GPS) antenna. Using satellites in space, the GPS can identify the tank's location anywhere on Earth.

Hull

A tank's turret is attached to the hull. While the gunner, commander, and loader work in the turret, the hull is home to the driver and the tank's engine. The driver sits at the front of the hull so he can see to steer the tank and control its speed.

The driver steers with handlebars that control the speed of the tracks on either side of the tank. To make a tank turn left, the right track goes faster and the left track goes slower. With this kind of steering, a tank can turn completely around in a tight circle by having one track go forward while the other track goes backward.

The front of the hull has a small opening, or hatch, beneath the swinging barrel of the main gun. Through the hatch, the driver can see outside, straight down the slanting flat armor plate called the glacis. When the tank is buttoned up, he can look outside through one of three periscopes. Sometimes, the glacis and the tank's bottom front armor, called the chin, must support a plow used for moving land mines. These are bombs that explode when the weight of the tank rolls over them or a soldier steps on them.

The rear of the hull holds the sturdy tank engine that drives the tracks and provides electrical power. Because the tank weighs 70 tons (140,000 pounds, or 63,503 kilograms), the engine must be very powerful. A 1,500-hp engine does the trick. (For comparison, a large SUV has about a 250-hp engine.) This powerful engine must be able to run at 30 to 40 mph (48–64 kph) for hours at a time. It must also be able to run without overheating while the tank is stopped.

Air is used to cool the engine and is also piped through the tank for the crew. A special air filter system cleans the air and keeps it free of road dust and smoke. It also keeps any nuclear radiation or chemical gas from entering the tank and warns the crew with an alarm if harmful air does get in. Every tank has special chemical-resistant suits stored for each crewman.

The tank's hull is watertight like a boat and can roll through water as deep as 6.5 feet (2 meters).

Measuring with Millimeters

The end of a rifle barrel is called the muzzle. The diameter of the barrel inside the muzzle is measured in millimeters (mm). Gun barrels are made to accept shells or bullets of one size only, based on the diameter of the barrel. For example, a 75mm gun uses only 75mm ammunition in its 75mm muzzle. (That is about three inches in diameter.) The M1A2 Abrams tank fires 120mm ammunition through its main gun barrel. (This is about four and three-quarter inches.)

Tracks

Without its tracks, a tank is only a big armored box with guns. Also called treads, tracks are what make the tank unique on the battle-field.

Every tank has two tracks, one on each side of the hull. A track is made up of many track blocks, which are built from steel plates and rubber. The track blocks are connected with hinges. The connected track blocks are wrapped around the tank's wheels to form a loop.

At the rear of the tank is a pair of large wheels with teeth, called sprocket wheels, that fit into spaces between the track blocks. These sprocket wheels are turned by the engine. In turn, the sprocket wheels move the track blocks like a bicycle chain. Torsion bars between each wheel and the hull act like springs and flex with every bump in the road.

A track broken in battle can stop a tank. That is why some armored fighting vehicles (AFVs) have armor panels called skirts to protect the tracks.

Unlike the past, today's battlefields often have no front line, where large numbers of soldiers move in one direction against the opposing side. Instead, today's military commanders must be able to attack in any direction at any time. They must be able to send soldiers and guns quickly to meet attacks. Modern AFV teams meet that battlefield challenge.

Global Positioning System (GPS)

Now in use by hundreds of millions of people in their phones, watches, and cars, the Global Positioning System (GPS) was developed by the Department of Defense in the 1970s to provide critical navigation capabilities to the military. It became fully operational in 1995 and is a space-based satellite navigation system that provides location and time information in all weather conditions, anywhere on or near Earth where there is an unobstructed line of sight to four or more GPS satellites. It is owned and operated by the US government.

A US Air Force captain explains how to use a GPS instrument to Afghan pilots from the Afghan National Army Air Corps.

On the Way!
The M60A1 Patton

On February 24, 1991, in the middle of Operation Desert Storm, the US Marines were on their way to free the nation of Kuwait, which had been invaded by Iraq. The Iraqi army had built huge hills of sand called berms to block the attack.

With their M60A1 Patton tanks leading the way, rumbling into the desert night, squads of marines went along with the tanks, protected inside Armored Assault Vehicles (AAVs). The leading M60A1 tanks had large plows, which they used to push aside the berms. Other M60A1s had plows that dug up land mines and cleared paths for the marine AAVs. Soon, the battle tanks rolled forward, firing their main guns and machine guns at opposing positions.

Behind clouds of chemical smoke, the powerful T-72 tanks of the Iraqi army tried to fight back. The marine M60A1 tanks were older

M60A1 tanks had bigger guns and thicker armor than the M48 tanks they replaced.

and had less powerful guns. But the American tanks had equipment that allowed their crews to see in the dark.

As the drivers steered the marine tanks over the sand, commanders located the targets and gunners aimed the guns. The loaders called out that the guns were ready to fire. In turn, the gunners yelled "On the way!" and squeezed the triggers.

One after another the marine M60A1s fired, and exploding Iraqi tanks lit up the night. By morning the Iraqi tank crews surrendered. Marines poured from the AAVs to capture the opposing soldiers without firing another shot. Cheering crowds of civilians greeted the marine tankers in their "old" Pattons as the tanks were the first to roll in to free the people of Kuwait City.

FACT

General George S. Patton Jr.

The M48 through M60A1 tanks were named for General George S. Patton Jr. (1885–1945). Patton had been a pioneer armored tank commander in the 1930s. His command of the US Army in Europe during World War II had M4 Sherman tanks slicing through German lines of defense, cutting off the opposing troops from their supplies and capturing thousands of German soldiers.

General George S. Patton Jr.

M46s were used during the Korean War. They were first replaced by M48s, followed by M60A1s and M1A1s.

The first Patton tanks were designed in the late 1940s. By the end of World War II in 1945, it was clear that the United States had to replace the M4 Sherman tank with something new. While the M4 had served well, newer tanks designed by Germany and the Soviet Union were faster and more durable. By 1949, the M46 Patton was designed in time for the Korean War (1950–1953). It outdid the Soviet Union's best tank in armor and firepower. The M46 tank was steadily improved until 1953, when it was replaced by the M48. The long-lived M48 was sold to countries throughout the world that appreciated its versatility.

The M48 Patton was a well-designed tank that fought in both the Korean and Vietnam conflicts from the 1950s through the 1970s. By 1956, however, the Soviet Union, America's rival at the time, had produced the T-54 tank with heavy armor and a big gun. A new

American tank design was needed, and the M60A1 Patton was the result.

This new tank came out in 1963. It weighed 58 tons (52.6 metric tons), was 21 feet (6.4 m) long and 11 feet (3.3 m) wide, and had a top speed of 30 mph (48 kph). It also had a bigger gun, thicker armor, and a new V-12 750-hp diesel engine. This was the first time American tank designers used a diesel engine instead of one that ran on gasoline. Diesel fuel does not burn as easily as gasoline if struck by a shell.

During Operation Desert Storm, these tanks from the 1960s were still in use, but they carried many new features. The most important one was the ability to see and shoot in the dark. Another improvement was new armor placed over the tank's regular armor. The new armor was called explosive reactive armor (ERA). It was made to explode when hit.

High-explosive anti-tank (HEAT) ammunition is designed specifically to damage or destroy the tough tank armor. But when HEAT rounds hit ERA, the armor plates explode. This reduces the energy of the ammunition trying to burn a hole through the tank's hull. The ERA plates are made to overlap like shingles on a roof to ensure that the tank's vulnerable parts are protected.

Following its 1991 service in Operation Desert Storm, the M60A1 tanks were finally retired from the US Marine Corps and replaced by M1A1 Abrams tanks, having ably served the nation for thirty years.

Seeing in the Dark

A new system for aiming guns was developed late in World War II and improved during the Vietnam War. Called thermal imaging, it allowed marine tankers to see in the dark by detecting the heat given off by opposing troops and tank engines. Each target appeared as a "signature" on a viewing screen in the M60A1. In today's thermal imagers, these signatures appear as different bright colors, depending on the heat of the objects in them. A hot tank engine is bright red or pink, while cooler trees or water are green or blue.

The thermal imaging sights of a tank reveal M1A1 Abrams tank crews.

Modern Tanks in Action: The M1A2 Abrams

It was February 1991 near the Euphrates River in Iraq. An M1A2 Abrams tank was stuck in the mud. It was the height of Operation Desert Storm. Three Iraqi T-72 tanks were lingering nearby, ready to attack. Stranded and vulnerable to the enemy, the Abrams commander called in reinforcements.

Immediately, one T-72 tank fired a high-explosive anti-tank warhead, or HEAT round, into the Abrams's turret. The round bounced off the tank's explosive reactive armor, or ERA, the tank's protection against weapons. The Abrams commander turned the turret toward the opposing tank. Then the gunner pointed the tank's gun and fired, and the T-72 tank's turret exploded. The second Iraqi tank fired a HEAT round that also hit the Abrams turret. This round also harmlessly bounced off the steeply angled armor plate.

As the vibration and "gong" sound of the direct hit faded away, the Abrams's gunner again aimed the main gun and fired. With that, the second Iraqi tank blew apart. The third T-72 tank fired another round. This one bounced off the hull as well, leaving a dent in the Abrams's glacis armor.

The Iraqi tank sped past at top speed—about 37 mph (60 kph)—and hid behind a distant sand dune. With the thermal imaging gun sight, the Abrams's gunner saw the bright image of the tank's hot engine exhaust rising above the dune. His loader heaved another round into the main gun. The Abrams fired a third shot through the sand dune and exploded the Iraqi tank on the other side. The Abrams crew blew smoke from its gun barrel and continued to wait to be pulled from the mud.

Lethal and Agile

By the 1970s, the United States was once again behind its rivals in tank design. American designers had to come up with a new tank that would match the others in firepower, protection, and mobility.

They needed to design a tank with armor heavy enough to protect its crew, but with the ability to move fast. The tank also had to have a big enough gun to ensure success in battle. By using the latest armor, engine, and gun technology, they created a completely new kind of tank: the M1.

Recognized by countries around the world as the finest weapon of its kind, the M1 is named after US Army general Creighton Abrams. The design of this tank was very different from that of World War II tanks such as the M60A1. Since it was introduced, the Abrams has been improved twice. Today's Abrams tank is the M1A2.

The Abrams tank is 32 feet (9.7 m) long, made of armor slabs, and built low to the ground. While older tanks like the M60A1 stand tall at 12 feet (3.6 m) with rounded curves, the Abrams looks as if it has been squashed down to its 8-foot (2.4-m) height. But its skin is harder than steel. Sheets of steel armor up to 11 inches (28 centimeters) thick are combined with sheets of special ceramic sealed between more sheets of steel and welded together. Bullets, rockets, grenades, and most HEAT rounds slide off those angled slabs of armor.

The tracks of the Abrams are almost 50 feet (15.2 m) long, made up of seventy-nine metal links padded with rubber. The rubber feet

The US Army's main battle tank is the M1A2 Abrams.

make the Abrams very quiet. Its engine is also quiet, but it is so powerful that the Abrams can go from zero to 20 mph (32 kph) in six seconds. In a few seconds more, it is churning along at 40 mph (64 kph). That is not bad for a vehicle that weighs as much as fifty cars! At 30 mph (48 kph), an Abrams can stop in a little less than 10 feet (3 m). The M1A2 can also fire at and destroy as many as six targets, some up to two miles (3.2 km) away, in less than a minute. The soldiers who fight alongside the Abrams tanks call them "whispering death."

During Operation Iraqi Freedom, starting in 2003, Abrams tanks traveled long distances, sometimes up to 265 miles (426 km), before refueling. While making the "Thunder Run" on April 5, 2003, outside Baghdad, the tanks had to keep fuel trucks close by. The M1A2 has a 505-gallon (1,912-liter) fuel tank, but it gets only 0.6 miles (1 km) to the gallon. This means that the tank can go only about 300 miles (480 km) on one tank of gas. It takes brave soldiers to drive fuel and ammunition trucks to keep up with the tanks.

An Abrams crew's battle stations inside the tank are "air-conditioned," but they are not pleasantly cool. They get as warm as 96 degrees Fahrenheit (35.5 degrees Celsius), and the metal surfaces of electronic equipment can get as hot as 126 degrees Fahrenheit (52.2 degrees Celsius) to the touch. The tank's engines together with jungle or desert heat can keep things sizzling.

With the tank buttoned up, the commander keeps in contact with his crew and platoon through an Intervehicle Information System (IVIS) radio. He also has a Position Navigation (POS/NAV) system connected by antenna to GPS satellites. This system helps guide the tank as it travels from point A to point B using information from the GPS. Both the commander and the gunner have Independent Thermal Viewers (ITV) to see heat reflected by objects and people at night or in bad weather conditions.

The gunner types into a computer the kind of ammunition being fired, the outside temperature, and other information. The computer checks the wind speed from a sensor on the tank's roof.

Army personnel load their M1A2 Abrams tank onto a train car.

It checks for the slight droop of the main gun's long barrel and the tilt of the tank if it is not on flat ground. After it has checked all of these things, the computer tells the gunner when he is on target and that the gun is ready to fire. The gunner calls out "On the way!" and fires. If he is unable to aim and fire the gun, the commander can aim and fire the gun from his position higher in the turret. Near the gunner, the loader wears heavy gloves as he heaves explosive rounds from a rack that is protected by a sliding steel panel. The loader also fires a machine gun mounted on the turret roof. If the Abrams gets damaged, a sliding steel shield protects the ammunition from fire.

In Operation Desert Storm, Abrams tanks destroyed 2,500 Iraqi tanks and armored vehicles. No Abrams tanks were lost to opposing gunfire and only 18 suffered battle damage. Not a single Abrams crewman was killed in action. During Operation Iraqi Freedom, as many as 40 Abrams tanks were damaged by rocket-propelled grenades (RPGs). Most were repaired and put back in action within a week.

General Creighton Abrams

Many people think that General Creighton Abrams (1914–1974) was one of the army's greatest fighting generals. During World War II, he commanded the 37th Tank Battalion, 4th Armored Division, which led the army's advance across France into Germany. He was a fearless and fierce leader in combat. General Abrams became the commanding officer of the entire US Army in 1972. He was the first leader of armored forces to hold that job.

General Creighton Abrams with his troops in Vietnam, 1968.

The Tank That Almost Failed

The M1 Abrams tank was designed in the 1970s as a new type of tank. But many people thought it would be a failure. They thought that it used too much fuel and that its engine would burn easily if the tank were attacked. The tank seemed to work well at the National Training Center (NTC), a huge desert area in Southern California. How the tank would work in combat might be a different story. But the M1A1 Abrams surprised everyone when it took charge of the battlefield and led to a quick victory over the Iraqi army in Operation Desert Storm.

M1A1 Abrams tank

Safe and Reliable Transportation:

The Bradley Fighting Vehicle

The armored-plate sides and roof began to rattle as machine-gun fire rained over an armored column of vehicles on their way to capture the Baghdad airport in April 2003. But instead of outrunning the gunfire, the convoy of vehicles was stopped while it waited for a special Bradley Fighting Vehicle (BFV) to arrive. Inside one of the vehicles lay the commander of one of the Bradleys, seriously wounded and awaiting evacuation.

Rushing at top speed past Abrams tanks and other BFVs stopped on this dangerous highway, this special BFV was outfitted to be an Armored Medical Evacuation Vehicle (AMEV), or ambulance.

The driver stopped his AMEV between the gunfire and the wounded commander. Suddenly, an RPG exploded against the top hatch of a nearby Bradley and an American soldier crashed to the pavement with burns and a broken leg.

The Abrams tanks and Bradleys doubled their return fire at the gunmen as the medics ran through the hail of bullets to carry the second wounded soldier into the armored ambulance. With bullets and grenades smashing into it, the AMEV turned and sped away, taking the two wounded men to a medical helicopter. The armored column, with guns firing, rumbled along on its mission.

The mission of the Bradley Fighting Vehicle is to provide safe and reliable transportation for soldiers to locations on the battlefield. The Bradley, however, is much more than a "battlefield taxi." It is armed so its crew can defend itself and the soldiers it carries. It can defeat opposing tanks and other fighting vehicles. It is fast enough to keep up with Abrams tanks and has powerful weapons that can defeat almost any opposing force. It can be used in many different ways, from attacking an opposing force to transporting wounded soldiers.

The Bradley Fighting Vehicle is named after General Omar Bradley, an officer who earned the love and respect of his men in World War II. He tried to stay close to his soldiers so he always knew what was going on in the front lines. General Bradley believed in striking swiftly and powerfully, like the BFV.

This vehicle has a crew of three: commander, driver, and gunner. It is designed to carry up to eight additional soldiers into combat protected by its two machine guns and armor. It was developed in 1981 to replace the lightly armed and armored M113 tracked troop carrier that had been used in the Vietnam War.

The M2 Bradley is as much a dangerous weapon as a troop carrier. Its main gun is the M242 25mm "Bushmaster" Chain Gun. The gunner may fire it one shot at a time or 200 shots per minute as a machine gun. To protect the BFV from an opposing main battle tank, two missiles are attached to the side of the Bradley's turret. These guided missiles are powerful weapons that can fly up to one mile (1.6 km). They can punch through up to 30 inches (76 cm) of armor. That is two and a half feet (.76 m) thick!

A column of M-2 Bradley armored vehicles

The latest version of the Bradley is the M2A3. It has digital display screens that allow the commander to automatically follow a target as it moves, adjust the gun, and aim it on the target before firing.

Bradley Fighting Vehicles can be transformed for many different uses. One of the most important is the AMEV. To turn a Bradley into an ambulance, the turret is taken off, the roof is raised thirteen inches (33 cm), and the fuel tanks are moved to the outside. This makes the inside of the Bradley large enough for a medical crew, their lifesaving equipment, and up to eight wounded soldiers, both lying down and sitting up. The AMEV crew provides lifesaving combat medical help for wounded soldiers. At the same time, the medical crew is protected by the AMEV. Inside the armored vehicle, the crew can work safely on injured soldiers while it speeds away from the battlefield to a military hospital.

The Bradley can travel at 40 mph (64 kph) with its turbo-diesel engine, keeping up with the speedy Abrams tank. Together they bring firepower and fighting men to the battlefield.

FACT

The Bradley Command and Control Vehicle (C2V)

The Bradley C2V is a special vehicle that keeps up with armored forces. It carries and protects the commanding officer and his staff. The C2V has wireless communications systems so the commanding officer can be in control of his entire armored force. The C2V's hull can be made into a fire control center, which locates targets and directs tank fire to those targets. From a C2V a commander can control forces right there in the field where situations change suddenly and decisions need to be made quickly.

Tanks and Troops Need Support

During Operation Iraqi Freedom in 2003, American forces, including the tank crews, needed a constant supply of food, ammunition, and medical equipment. The troops call this "beans, bullets, and band-aids." Special fuel for the Abrams tanks had to be transported over dangerous roads. Supplies such as ammunition, food, spare tank parts, clothing, and thousands of gallons of drinking water were also brought in.

The job of supplying all these soldiers and vehicles is called logistics. The job is done by the Headquarters Unit, a communications and battle-planning center set up at the rear of the fighting, where supplies are stored. The men and women in charge of logistics make sure the tanks and their crews have everything they need.

The Bradley M6 Linebacker

The M6 is designed to defend against attacks from opposing aircraft. The Linebacker, as the M6 is known, is a Bradley Fighting Vehicle fitted with Stinger surface-to-air missiles. These four guided missiles allow the Linebacker to fire at aircraft while on the move (on the ground, or "surface"). They also protect an armored unit by day or night.

An M2A2 Bradley Fighting Vehicle leaves for a mission in Iraq.

Alternative Fuels Save Lives

All vehicles used in combat run on gasoline, which has to be imported and delivered to very remote areas where the military is fighting. These convoys of delivery trucks are highly vulnerable to attacks by insurgents and improvised explosive devices (IEDs). The less fuel that the Humvees, tanks, and MRAPs use, the less frequently these delivery trucks have to make these dangerous trips. So, the military is increasingly employing alternative fuels like solar power. One marine company that installed solar panels in the Helmand Province in Afghanistan reduced its fuel consumption by 90 percent!

So You Want to Be an Armor Crewman?

The battle tank is a complex weapon designed to bring heavy firepower to a battle and crash through opposing forces, destroying their will to fight. Armor crewmen are up to the challenge, but training to become one requires hard work.

An armor crewman must be in excellent physical condition and have a lot of energy and strength for lifting, repairing steel and rubber track blocks, lugging heavy tow chains, and tightening bolts with large wrenches. Everything in a tank is heavy. There is ammunition to load, and each shell weighs between 50 and 60 pounds (22–27 kg). The Abrams holds forty shells. Hatch covers, made of 2-inch (5-cm) armored steel, have to be heaved open and locked closed.

An armor crewman must be able to work inside a stuffy tank for days at a time, sometimes at temperatures of 90 degrees Fahrenheit

(32 degrees Celsius). Good vision is needed in order to read maps, drive vehicles around obstacles, and locate targets.

In addition to their physical conditioning, each crewman must be able to work as part of a team and be ready to face danger. The ability to stay calm when bullets and bombs are clanging off the tank's armor is very important for battlefield survival.

Job training for an armor crewman begins with basic training. Here, recruits learn basic soldiering skills such as marching, wearing uniforms, obeying orders, and firing small arms. They also learn teamwork—how to work with others to finish a job. Another thing they learn is how to live by the military code of conduct, a set of rules that must be followed to ensure the honor of the military and the safety of fellow soldiers.

After basic training there are three to four months of special training for those who want to become armor crewmen.

The US Army and Marine Corps have many training centers for armor crewmen. The army has the largest armored post in the United States at Fort Hood, Texas. Soldiers at Fort Hood train with the latest weapons and computer-based technology.

In a classroom, the armor crewmen students learn how to operate the tank, how to attack, and how to defend their tank. They learn to read battlefield maps that show the steepness of hills, depth of water, and details about features such as railroads, towns, and bridges. The students learn how to search for the opposing side without being detected. They study how tanks are used by commanders in many kinds of combat situations to understand their part in a battle.

When they are not in a classroom, students are in the field taking part in war games, fighting simulated battles with real tanks. Tank crew students can also fight simulated tank battles indoors using computer-operated Close Combat Tactical Trainers (CCTTs).

Close Combat Tactical Trainers are exact copies of the inside of Abrams and Bradley vehicles. Students work inside these trainers using realistic, computer-generated combat simulations similar to

US Army training involves physical exercise and hands-on vehicle training.

video games. These simulations help them learn how tanks operate in battle.

Hands-on armored vehicle training includes learning how to repair tanks in the field and requires mechanical skills. Changing engine parts, fixing broken tracks, repairing jammed machine guns, and changing the tank's oil are all important skills to know in a combat zone. All soldiers must know how to do each of these jobs. They must be familiar with every electrical and mechanical system in their tanks.

Firsthand experience working on and operating tanks and their equipment is good preparation for careers in engineering and automobile and mechanical repair. Armor crewmen learn teamwork, discipline, and how to accept responsibility. These important skills will help in any career after military service.

Armor crewmen have the know-how and stamina to operate these intimidating weapons. They are part of a hardworking team that lives and fights inside some of the fiercest weapons to be found in any battle zone.

Tank Crews
Need Rifles Too

Besides loading and firing the cannons and machine guns, each armor crewman on an Abrams tank is assigned a rifle to take into combat. The army M4 rifle was chosen because the inside of the tank has very little extra room. The M4 is the same as a standard M16 soldier's rifle, but the M4's shoulder stock collapses like a telescope and the barrel is shorter, to take up less space. The M4 can fire one shot or all thirty of its rounds with a single trigger squeeze.

Armor crewmen carry M4 rifles with them into combat.

Close Combat Tactical Trainers

Close Combat Tactical Trainers (CCTTs) help armored units get ready for combat. Inside the trainers, crewmen sit in front of computer screens that show views they would see through periscopes in a buttoned-up tank. They train to do their jobs in deserts, jungles, and cities.

The CCTT can imitate actual battlefield conditions on the students' view screens while the students practice operating weapons amid the whine of the engine, the rumble of the treads, and the boom of shells. Simulated rain and sand storms swirl across their view. They even feel the jolt of bumpy roads. All of this makes the training very realistic.

Trainers can create the kinds of environments crewmen are likely to live and fight in. CCTTs prepare crewmen and teach them information about operating a tank and other military vehicles that can save lives later, in actual combat. CCTTs are located at Fort Hood, Texas, and at other armor training schools.

Female Soldiers in Tanks

On January 24, 2013, then Secretary of Defense Leon Panetta removed the military's ban on women serving in combat. Since then, more than 70,000 positions that were previously closed to women have been opened. Army major Christina "Chrissy" Cook became the first woman in the 1st Cavalry Division to qualify on the Bradley Fighting Vehicle in July 2014.

Major Chrissy Cook sits in her Bradley Fighting Vehicle.

1914–1918—British deploy tanks in the trenches of World War I.

1939–1945—German tanks, or Panzers, are deployed in World War II.

1949—First Patton tank is introduced.

1980—First Abrams tank is introduced.

1981—First Bradley Fighting Vehicle is introduced.

M48 Patton

ammunition—An object, such as a bullet, that is fired from a weapon.

glacis—A sloped slab of armor at the front of a tank's hull, similar to the hood of a car.

grenade—A small explosive weapon thrown by hand or fired from a special type of gun.

hatch—A small door or opening in a tank.

hull—The main body of a tank.

logistics—Locating, moving, and storing supplies.

periscope—A tool that uses lenses and mirrors to reflect the image of an object hidden from view.

shell—Ammunition shot from a cannon that explodes when it hits its target.

simulation—Imitation of a real battle that allows an armored crewman trainee to take part with less risk of danger.

sprocket wheels—Wheels at the rear of a tank with steel teeth that fit into slots on the tank's tracks. They help to move the tracks.

thermal imaging—Technology that allows tanker crews to see in the dark by detecting the heat given off by opposing troops and tank engines.

torsion bars—Bars between each tank wheel and the hull that twist when the tracks roll over bumps and act like springs to help make the ride smoother for the crew.

track blocks—Sections of a tank's tracks. They are made of thick rubber to grip the ground or the road.

tracks—Also called treads. Connected steel and rubber track blocks that loop over a tank's wheels and keep the tank in constant contact with the ground while traveling over rough terrain.

turret—A revolving tower at the top of a tank. It is made of thick armored plates and can rotate and move the main gun in a circle.

FURTHER READING

BOOKS

Hamilton, John. *Abrams Tanks.* Minneapolis, Minn.: ABDO & Daughters, 2011.

Hamilton, John. *Bradley Fighting Vehicles.* Minneapolis, Minn.: ABDO & Daughters, 2011.

Haskew, Michael. *The World's Greatest Tanks: An Illustrated History.* London: Amber Books, 2014.

Von Finn, Denny. *Strykers.* Minneapolis, Minn.: Bellwether Media, 2014.

WEB SITES

military.com/equipment/m1126-stryker-combat-vehicle
Information Web site on Stryker vehicles

military.com/video/combat-vehicles/combat-tanks/nothing-stops-a-tank/4032268151001
Watch tank videos

nationalinfantrymuseum.org
The National Infantry Museum.

INDEX